Woodland Animals

A ZEBRA BOOK

Written by Wendy Boase
Illustrated by Peter Visscher

PUBLISHED BY
WALKER BOOKS
LONDON

This is a snail. He likes
to sleep near some moss.

This is a weasel sleeping
under a hazel bush.

This is a deer. He likes
to sleep in the bracken.

This is a fox curled up
among the tree roots.

This is a moth. She likes
to sleep on dead leaves.

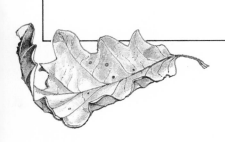

This is an owl. He likes
to sleep in a hollow tree.

When the sun goes down
all the animals
will wake up.

The snail comes out of his shell
and nibbles a mushroom.

The weasel is busy
looking for rabbits.

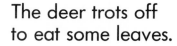

The deer trots off
to eat some leaves.

The fox slinks out
to hunt for mice.

The moth drinks nectar
from a flower.

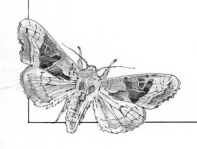

The owl swoops down
to catch a rat before
the sun comes up again.